WATER LIFE

NATURE'S • HIDDEN • WORLDS

WATER LIFE

Written by
CECILIA FITZSIMONS

Illustrated by
HELEN WARD

RSVP

RAINTREE
STECK-VAUGHN
PUBLISHERS
The Steck-Vaughn Company

Austin, Texas

Published by Raintree Steck-Vaughn, an imprint of Steck-Vaughn Company.

Library of Congress Cataloging-in-Publication Data

Fitzsimons, Cecilia

Water life / written by Cecilia Fitzsimons; illustrated by Helen Ward

p. cm. — (Nature's hidden worlds)

Includes index.

Summary: Examines various animals that live in or near the water, discussing such habitats as swamps, ponds, and the seashore.

ISBN 0-8172-3971-5 (Hardcover)

ISBN 0-8172-4185-X (Softcover)

1. Aquatic animals—Juvenile literature. 2. Aquatic habitats—Juvenile literature

[1. Aquatic animals.] I. Ward, Helen, 1962-   . II. Title. III. Series.

QL 120.F576 1996   95-18859

591.92—dc20   CIP AC

Note to reader

There are some words in this book that are printed in **bold** type. You will find the meanings for each of these words in the glossary on page 46.

Designer: Mike Jolley

Project Editor: Wendy Madgwick

Editor: Kim Merlino

Printed in Italy

1 2 3 4 5 6 7 8 9 LB 99 98 97 96

Introduction

Nearly three-quarters of the Earth's surface is covered by water. This book shows some of the wildlife living in or near the water. Each picture involves a puzzle. Which baby turtle will reach the sea? Spot the differences between two pictures of a tide pool. Match up an animal with its home. As you solve the puzzles you will learn about life in the ocean and fresh water.

Contents

1

Swamp Life

Many coasts in tropical areas are covered by forests of mangrove trees. Several different kinds of animals live in mangrove swamps. Look carefully at these two pictures of a mangrove swamp in Southeast Asia. Can you spot the ten differences between them?

The mouth of a river where it flows into the sea is called an **estuary**. Many estuaries are bordered by mudflats. Wildlife living here has to cope with two main problems. The tide flowing in and out, and the mix of fresh and salt water.

In hot, tropical countries, mangrove trees grow along the estuary. They are one of the few trees that can grow in salt water.

Mangrove trees have large roots to support them in the soft mud. These roots are called prop or **stilt roots**. Some mangroves have short roots that stick up out of the mud, into the air. These **aerial roots** help the tree to take in oxygen from the air.

In the Mud

Did you spot the ten differences?

1 Another mudskipper is climbing a mangrove root.

2 The archer fish is shooting a jet of water.

3 One fiddler crab now has a large claw.

4 A ghost crab has come out of its burrow.

5 The saltwater crocodile's mouth is open.

6 A long-tailed macaque is holding a crab.

7 An indian darter (snake bird) has a fish in its beak.

8 An egret is in a tree.

9 One mangrove winkle is missing.

10 The mangrove snake has changed position.

Other animals in the picture:

11 Mangrove oyster.

12 Tentacled snake.

13 Proboscis monkey.

8

Snake birds

Mangrove swamps are home to many kinds of birds. One of the most unusual is the darter, or snake bird. The snake bird feeds on fish. It stabs them with its sharp beak. While fishing, it swims with its body under the water. But its head and long neck are held above the surface. It looks just like a snake. After fishing, the snake bird stands on the shore. It holds its wings out to dry.

Along the shore, mud gets trapped between the mangrove roots. A swamp develops. Many different animals live here. Clusters of mangrove oysters grow on the tree roots. Mangrove winkles feed on the mud. When the tide comes in, they crawl up tree roots to safety. Small fish called mudskippers use their fleshy fins to crawl out onto the mud. They can even climb up into the mangrove trees. The male fish guard their **territories** on the mudflats. They use their raised dorsal fin to signal to the females.

The mudflats are also home to many kinds of crabs. Ghost crabs and fiddler crabs live in watertight **burrows** in the mud. The male fiddler crab has one small feeding claw and one huge claw. It may use the large one to attract a female or warn off a rival male. The crabs are hunted by long-tailed macaque monkeys and birds like egrets.

Other animals live in the trees. Proboscis monkeys feed in the tree tops, eating leaves, flowers, and fruit. Mangrove snakes coil through the branches searching for **prey**.

The tentacled snake is a sea snake. It hunts prey in the muddy waters. The archer fish catches its food in a special way. If it sees an insect on a leaf above it, the fish takes aim. It shoots out a jet of water to knock the insect into the swamp. The fish then gobbles it up!

The saltwater crocodile is the largest **predator** of the swamp. This rare animal is now protected in many areas.

2

Ponds and Lakes

Many animals rear their young in or near ponds and lakes. Look carefully at this picture of a large pond in North America. Can you match the young animals in the large picture with their parents shown in the small pictures? Look again. Can you see four more adults and their young in the main picture?

The fresh water of ponds and lakes swarms with fish and insect life. The water contains food for many kinds of animals. Tiny **algae**, too small to see, provide food for small grazing animals, such as snails. Leaves and other plant material rot in the water. They form a souplike mix called **detritus**. Small animals, such as worms, insects, and some fish, feed on this rotting mass. These animals in turn form food for other larger animals.

Many animals visit ponds to rear their young. Flying insects such as dragonflies lay their eggs in water.

Life in Fresh Water

Did you match the youngsters with their parents?

1 Raccoons washing their food.
2 A family of beavers.
3 Great blue heron chicks in a treetop nest.
4 Otter young, or kits, learning to fish.
5 Young muskrats on their feeding raft.

6 Young wood ducks on the water.
7 Leopard frog and tadpoles.
8 Green darner dragonfly and nymph.
9 Diving beetle and larva.
10 Brown trout with fry (young fish).

Fierce meat-eating **nymphs** with powerful jaws hatch out of the dragonfly eggs. Amphibians like frogs, toads, and salamanders return to water to lay their eggs. The tiny tadpoles that hatch are eaten by the **larvae** of the diving beetle. Tadpoles are also eaten by many fish including brown trout. The cycle continues, when the trout are in turn eaten by birds such as the belted kingfisher. Otters also feed on fish. Baby otters play together learning the skills that will make them good hunters.

Beavers live near lakes and feed on tree bark. They gnaw down young trees to build large dams and lodges to live in. Young beavers can swim soon after they are born. They stay with their parents for two years.

Muskrats look like beavers, but with flat, narrow tails. They eat water plants. Muskrats live on the banks of ponds in the rushes or in tunnels.

Raccoons live in woods near the water. They eat anything, including clams and turtles. Baby raccoons climb trees to escape their enemies.

The great blue heron and wood ducks nest in hollow tree holes. The fluffy, young wood ducks soon follow their mother onto the water.

Insects and their young

Many insects lay their eggs in water. The eggs hatch into young which may live in ponds and rivers for many years. The young insects grow by shedding their skin, or molting, many times. Some insect young feed on plants and detritus. Others, such as great diving beetles and dragonflies, are fierce predators.

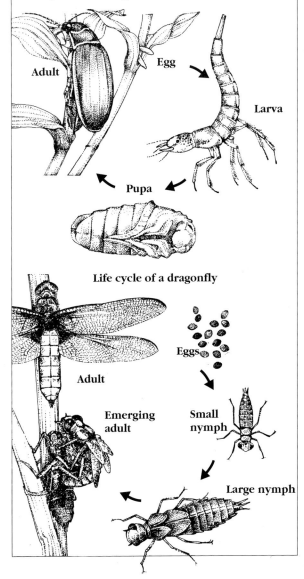

Life cycle of a diving beetle

Adult

Egg

Larva

Pupa

Life cycle of a dragonfly

Adult

Eggs

Emerging adult

Small nymph

Large nymph

3

The Coral Reef

A coral reef is home to a wealth of life. Thousands of different kinds of animals live here. Many are brightly colored. Other animals are not so easily seen. Look carefully at this picture of the Great Barrier Reef in Australia. Can you find the ten creatures hiding there?

Coral reefs only grow in the clear, shallow waters of warm tropical seas. These ancient **habitats** are home to a variety of different animals. The corals themselves are living animals. Each rocky structure is made by groups, or **colonies**, of tiny creatures. Corals are related to sea anemones. The coral animals are called **polyps**.

The polyps contain microscopic algae within their cells. The algae may help to produce the chalky coral. Each species of coral is different in its shape and form. The reef is just like a forest, a mass of lumps, plates, and branches. Corals are often brightly colored, but there are dark crevices between them. The reefs are home to many fish.

Indonesia

Great Barrier Reef

Australia

The Great Barrier Reef

Coral reefs are found only in the tropics. They grow in shallow waters, near coastlines and around islands. The Great Barrier Reef is so large that it can be seen from space. The Great Barrier Reef is not a single reef. It is a whole system of reefs more than 1,250 miles (2,000 km) long. They lie along the northeast coast of Australia. Scientists think that this reef began growing about 15–18 million years ago. The present-day living reef has been growing for about 8,000 years.

Underwater Forests

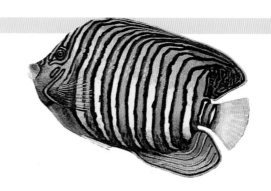

Brightly colored angel fish (A) and lionfish (B) are easy to see as they swim along. The striped clownfish (C) hides among the tentacles of a stinging anemone. The blue-ringed octopus (D) hides in rocky crevices waiting for passing prey. Cobalt blue starfish (E) and giant clams (F) add to this colorful scene.

Not all the fish in the coral reef are so easy to spot. Butterfly fish, trigger fish, and Moorish idols swim between the coral's branches. Their bodies are striped and spotted with bright and dark colors. This **camouflage** makes the fish hard to see in the coral. They look like both the bright coral and the dark shadows in between.

Playing hide and seek

Hidden animals:
1 Golden butterfly fish.
2 Wobegong or carpet shark.
3 Tiger cowrie.
4 Frogfish.
5 Moorish idol.
6 Trigger fish.
7 Red rock cod.
8 Stonefish.
9 Painted crayfish.
10 Banded sea snake.

The ocean floor is often covered with pebbles and broken coral. Other fish hide among the rocks or lie partly buried in the sand. The wobegong is a type of shark that lives on the seabed. Its wide, flat body blends in with the rocks. The frog fish and red rock cod are hard to see. They look like the seaweed-covered rocks they hide between.

A stonefish is also camouflaged to look like seaweed-covered rocks. But it also has another means of defense, a poisonous spine on its back.

This can badly hurt anything that treads on the stonefish.

The tiger cowrie has a beautiful, shiny shell. It feeds on algae at night. Its shell is covered by a skin called the mantle. This skin is patterned and covered in tentacles. The cowrie looks like a weed-covered pebble, too.

The painted crayfish also feeds at night. During the day it is hard to see since it hides in a rocky crevice. The banded sea snake is sometimes seen on the reef. Its striped skin helps it blend in among the corals.

The living coral

The living coral is made up of thousands of coral polyps. Each polyp is a tiny animal, with a mouth surrounded by tentacles. The polyp looks like a sea anemone. Its tentacles sweep bits of food toward the polyp's mouth. As the polyps grow, they add chalky material to the skeleton of the coral beneath them. So new coral reefs grow on top of the old reefs.

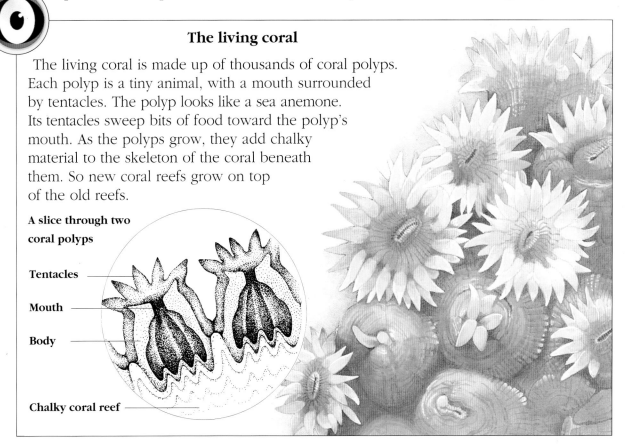

A slice through two coral polyps

Tentacles

Mouth

Body

Chalky coral reef

Ocean Depths

Many strange creatures live in the deepest oceans. No light can reach this deep below the surface. So no algae, such as seaweeds, can grow here. Look at this picture. Can you spot the ten animals or seaweeds that could not live in the dark depths?

Very little sunlight reaches below about 650 feet (200 m). By 3,000 feet (about 900 m) it is totally dark and cold. Some living things, such as green **plankton** and seaweeds, need sunlight to grow. This means that they cannot live in deep water. The only light found here is made by deep-sea animals.

The animals that live in the deep sea are adapted to survive in the dark and cold. Many deep-sea animals are blind. Smell, touch, and hearing are important. Food is scarce, so most animals grow slowly and only reach a small size.

Animals that make their own light use it in different ways. Some use it to attract their prey. Others flash the lights on their bodies to send messages to one another.

Other animals, such as whales, fish, and shrimp, make noises. They use these sounds to communicate with one another.

Another problem of living deep in the ocean is the weight of water above. The water presses on the animals. The pressure of the water increases the deeper you go. Deep-sea animals have a high pressure inside their bodies. This keeps them from collapsing under the pressure of the water.

Lighting the dark

Deep-sea fish have light-producing organs called photophores. A chemical reaction in the photophore produces a blue-green glowing light.

A Dark, Cold World

There are great changes in water pressure from the surface to the ocean floor. This means that few animals can safely travel between the surface and the deep. Despite this, air-breathing sperm whales (A) can dive to about 3,500 feet (1,000 m) in search of their prey, giant squid (B). Lantern fish are one of the few deep-sea **species** to visit the surface. Schools of these tiny fish are lifted by moving water currents to feed on plankton at the surface.

In the ocean depths, animals can only eat each other or detritus. Detritus is the dead remains that fall down from the surface waters above. Many predators, such as hatchet fish (C) and bristlemouth fish (D), have long sharp teeth to catch their prey.

Did you find the animals or seaweeds that cannot live in the deep ocean?

1 Kelp, a seaweed, cannot live in the dark.
2 Flying fish live in surface waters.
3 Walruses live on the seashore and in surface waters.
4 Penguins cannot live in deep water.
5 Damsel fish live in coral reefs. They cannot live in deep water.
6 Turtles usually live in shallow coastal waters.
7 Goldfish can only live in fresh water.
8 Staghorn coral grows on coral reefs.
9 Dragonfly nymphs live in freshwater ponds and rivers.
10 Murex snails live in shallow coastal seas.

The hatchet fish attracts its prey with lights. Most deep-sea animals are black and will show up in the light the fish makes. But some deep-sea prawns (E) and other soft-bodied animals are bright red. They look black in the blue-green light made by the hatchet fish. So these animals escape because they are very hard for the hatchet fish to see.

Other deep-sea fish have different ways of catching prey. Gulper eels (F) have huge heads and mouths to swallow their prey. Anglerfish (G) use a light on a stalk, just like a fishing rod. Unwary prey are attracted to the light. Instead they find a huge mouth! The rat tail (H) is a long-tailed fish related to cod. It detects its prey with its whiplike tail.

Other sea creatures, such as brittle stars, sea cucumbers, glass sponges, and worms, live on the ocean floor. Sea lilies and neopilina, a limpet, were known only as fossils. Then they were found in the deep ocean. Some tiny corals live here, too, but large reef corals cannot survive.

How deep is the ocean?

0 – 650 feet (0 – 200 m)
Shallow waters or benthic zone.
Sunlight filters through from the surface.

650 – 6,500 feet (200 – 2,000 m)
Continental slope or bathyal zone. This is like the side of the valley between shallow coastal waters and the deep ocean floor.

6,500 – 19,500 feet (2000 – 6,000 m)
Ocean floor or abyss. The deep ocean floor is a wide, flat plain that stretches between the continents.

19,500 – 36,000 feet (6,000 – 11,000 m)
Deep trench or hadal zone. Deep valleys or canyons cut through the ocean floor. So far, mostly soft-bodied animals have been found here.

5

River Life

Rivers and riverbanks are home to many different kinds of animals. Look carefully at this picture of a river in Northern Europe. Can you match the animals in the small pictures with their special home by or in the river?

A river starts its life as a stream of rain water that falls on mountains and hills. Other streams add more water along the way. Soon a small river is formed. The river gets larger and wider until eventually it empties into the sea or a large lake.

Mountain streams are fast-flowing and rocky. Very few plants live here. Animals have to swim strongly or cling to rocks to stop themselves from being swept away. Further downstream the river is slower and wider. Here many water plants can grow. They provide shelter and food for many kinds of animals.

The river and its bank are home to many birds that nest and feed here.

Home, Sweet Home

Homefinder

1   A kingfisher and its nest hole in the bank.

2   An otter and its hole with the entrance below the water.

3   A moorhen, or common gallinule, and its nest among water reeds.

4   A mute swan and its nest on a riverbank.

5   A water vole and its burrow with entrances above and below water.

6   An American mink and its den beneath the tree roots.

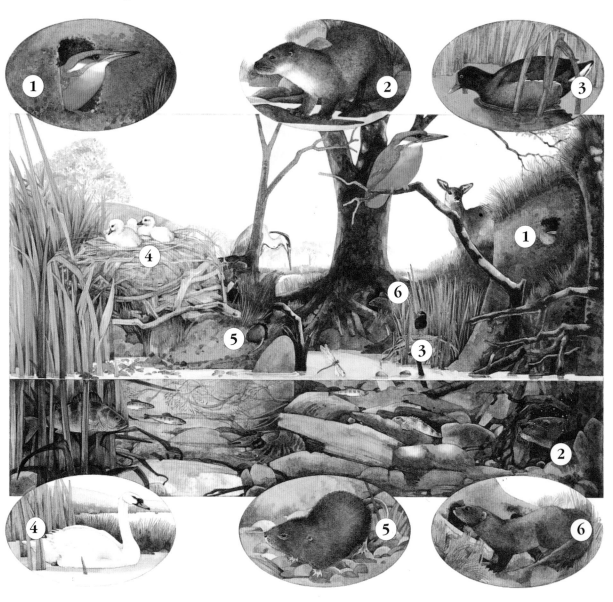

Kingfishers nest in riverbanks. They dig 3 feet- (1 m-) long tunnels in the banks. At the end of the tunnel is a round hole. Here the bird lays its eggs in a nest of fish bones.

Mute swans build their nests on top of a riverbank or in a weedy marsh. The nest is a huge pile of reeds and other weeds. It is lined with soft feathers. The male swan, called a cob, fiercely guards the nest and eggs. Moorhens, or common gallinules, build their nests among reeds at the water's edge.

Many mammals live on riverbanks. The otter is a rare water mammal. It is only found near quiet waterways. An otter's home is a large hole in a riverbank. The entrance can be above or below the water.

In Europe, the American mink was bred on fur farms for its skin. Some mink escaped. These fierce hunters now live in the wild. The mink has several well-hidden dens close to the water.

The tiny water vole feeds on grass. Its riverside burrow has entrances both above and below water.

Many different kinds of fish live in rivers and ponds. Perch, for example, swim between the reeds. The stripes on their sides make them hard to see among the reed stalks.

Swim, swim, swim

Most animals that live in rivers and streams are good swimmers. Many mammals push with their feet against the water when they swim. They use their feet like paddles. Mammals like otters and American mink have webbed hind feet to help them swim. Their webbed feet also help them to walk on the marshy riverbank.

Otter　　　　　　　　　　　　　**Water vole**

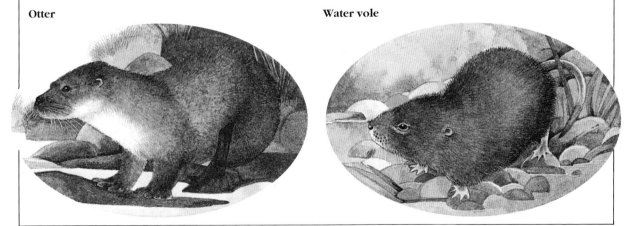

6

Beneath the Waves

The waters beneath the surface of the ocean are teaming with life. Look at these two pictures of life beneath the waves in the North Atlantic Ocean. Can you spot the ten differences between them?

The surface waters of the world's oceans are clear and bright. They are lit by the sun shining down from above. Billions of green one-celled living things grow in these sunny waters. These form the plantlike plankton. Tiny animal-like plankton feed on this green plankton. They in turn become food for larger animals.

Plankton is very important. It is the starting point for nearly all food chains in the ocean. Plankton is a very rich food and many tiny ocean creatures eat it. So do some of the largest animals. The biggest fish, whale sharks and basking sharks, and the largest mammals, baleen whales, eat only plankton.

A Wealth of Food

These sharks and whales strain large amounts of water through their mouths. The plankton is trapped on sievelike structures. The food is then wiped off and swallowed.

The basking shark also feeds on plankton. As it swims along at the surface, it filters its food from the water. These harmless sharks often grow to over 33 feet (10 m) long.

The tiny plankton are often carried along by the ocean current. Larger planktonic creatures, such as jellyfish, can drift for hundreds of miles. Long tentacles hang beneath their bodies. These are either sticky or have stinging cells. They are used to catch their prey.

Sunfish also drift lazily along in the surface currents. These strange fish are huge. Their round shape makes them look as if they have no body or tail. They catch jellyfish and other soft-bodied animals to eat.

Leatherback turtles also eat jellyfish. Sadly these endangered animals often die after eating plastic bags that they mistake for jellyfish. Plastic bags do not break down and can float in the ocean for months.

Schools of fish, such as mackerel, feed on planktonic shrimp called copepods. Gannets and other sea birds can see schools of fish from the air. They dive down and catch the fish with their daggerlike beaks.

Not-so-soft jellyfish

Jellyfish have soft bodies, although some can be tough and leathery. Most are a simple umbrella shape, with mouth, tentacles, and reproductive organs, called **gonads**, hanging below. The man-of-war is a colony of related animals that hang beneath a hollow, gas-filled sac. It floats on the surface of the ocean.

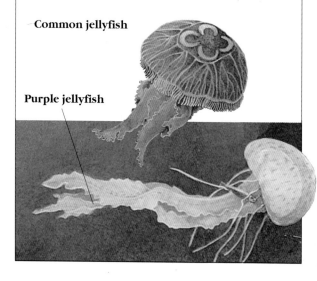

Common jellyfish

Purple jellyfish

Puffin catch small fish. When feeding its young, a puffin carries several small fish in its beak. The puffin's beak and mouth have backward-pointing spikes. These help grip the slippery fish. Puffins use their wings like paddles to "fly" underwater. The puffin's bill is only brightly striped during courtship. At other times it is gray.

Gray seals live in coastal waters. They dive for fish and shellfish to eat. Like all seals, their body is smooth and streamlined. Gray seals are very skillful swimmers. Their large eyes help them see well.

Common dolphins also hunt fish. They track and probably stun their prey with blasts of sound called **sonar**. In offshore waters, dolphins live in a large family group called a pod. They are often seen swimming by the side of ships. They ride the boat's waves just for fun.

Swimmers and floaters – the ten differences

1   The ocean sun fish is eating a jellyfish.

2   The position of the leatherback turtle's flipper is different.

3   The purple jellyfish has caught a fish in its tentacles.

4   The basking shark's mouth is now open and its red gills can be seen.

5   One of the mackerel is swimming in the opposite direction.

6   One of the gannets has a fish in its beak.

7   A common dolphin now has a dolphin pup.

8   The gray seal's back flippers are in a different position.

9   The common jellyfish now has a fourth reproductive organ called a gonad present.

10   A young puffin has been added.

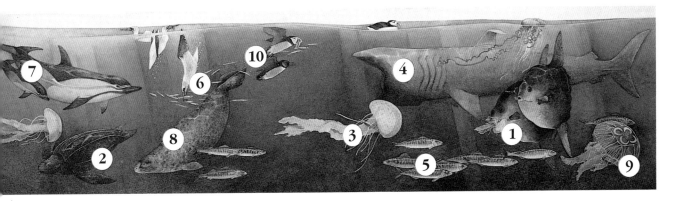

On the Seashore

Green turtles bury their eggs high up on a sandy beach. When the baby turtles (A) hatch, they must crawl back to the ocean. Look at this picture of a beach on the Florida coast. Follow the trails and find which turtles safely reached the water.

The seashore is the place where the land meets the sea. It is a habitat of sand, pebbles, rocks, or mud. Pebbles and rocks are found where the ocean is rough or currents are strong. Sand and mud is found in protected bays and estuaries.

Marine turtles spend their lives at sea. But the female must return to land to lay her eggs. She often returns to the sandy shore from which she hatched. The female green turtle digs a large hole with her front flippers. She lays about 100 hard-shelled eggs in the hole and covers them with sand.

About ten weeks later, the eggs hatch. The young turtles dig their way out. They struggle to climb out of the nest hole. The hatchlings flap their flippers as if trying to swim. They make their way down the beach to the ocean.

Young turtles mostly hatch at night. They are attracted to the moonlight reflected from the water. But many dangers bar their way.

Seashore birds

Egret

The seashore is home to many birds. Different species often feed on different food. The shape of a bird's beak will often tell you what it eats. An egret has a strong beak shaped like a dagger. It uses it to stab fish. A herring gull will eat almost anything. Its hook-shaped beak stops the fish it catches from slipping away. A dunlin has a long, thin beak. It searches in the sand or mud for worms.

Herring gulls

A

Pathways to the Ocean

On tourist beaches there are many bright lights. The young turtles are attracted to them. They crawl away from the water and many die. The hatchlings that come out at sunset or are still on the beach at dawn are in great danger. There are many predators waiting to pounce.

Birds such as herring gulls and egrets feed on the soft-shelled baby turtles. The frigate bird is a hunter, too. It swoops down and catches the hatchlings. Raccoons and domestic dogs sometimes join in the feast. They often dig up the eggs as well as feed on the young turtles.

The sandy beach is home to many other animals. Some of these feed on turtle eggs and hatchlings.

Important nest sites

Green turtles live in warm tropical waters all over the world. The most important nesting beaches are found on quiet islands. There are few predators on such islands. However, turtles also nest on many other beaches. Here the risks are much greater. The most important nesting sites are found in Costa Rica, on some tiny islands in the Caribbean, and on Ascension Island in the mid-Atlantic.

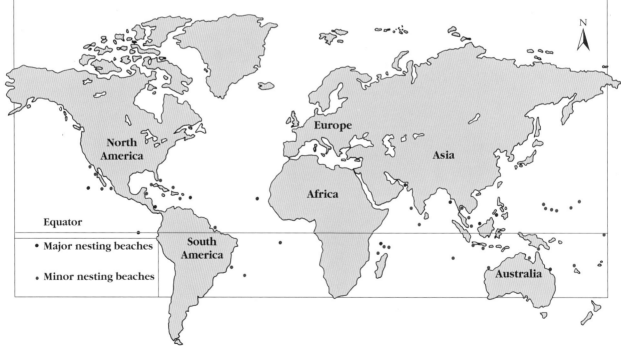

Ghost crabs lie hidden in sandy burrows. Only their long eyestalks can be seen above the sand. They usually feed on sand flies but will also attack newly hatched turtles. They catch them by a flipper and drag them underground. Square-bodied land crabs feed on both plants and animals.

The green turtle is a rare sight on the beach. Like most turtles, it has been hunted almost to extinction by people. Green turtles are now protected and should not be hunted.

Sadly, in some places, people still kill them for food and eat the eggs.

A sandy beach is home to many creatures. It may look empty, but millions of animals live beneath the surface. Worms, cockles and other clams, urchins, shrimps, crabs, and many others all burrow into the sand. They feed at high tide when the beach is covered with water.

At low tide, wading birds such as dunlin and oystercatchers feed. They use their long beaks to search in the sand for burrowing animals.

The great escape

1 Street lights attract the hatchlings away from the ocean.
2 Herring gulls feed on the hatchlings.
3 Ghost crabs will catch the young turtles.
4 Frigate birds swoop down and snatch up hatchlings.
5 Raccoons eat the young turtles and the eggs.
6 Domestic dogs eat the young turtles and eggs.
7 Egrets feed on the hatchlings.
8 Land crabs eat small animals and plants.

Other birds in the picture:
9 Dunlin.
10 Oystercatcher.

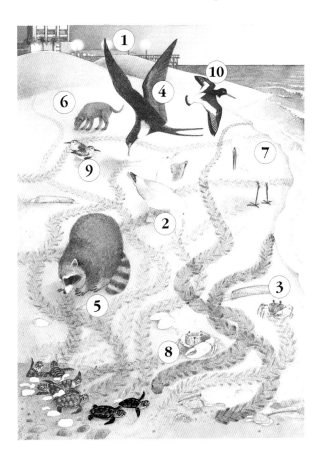

8
Wetlands

The flat marshes of Northern Europe are a safe home for many animals. Look carefully at this picture of a marsh. Can you find the ten animals that usually live in warmer parts of the world?

In flat wetland areas, rivers loop and twist as they slowly flow to the ocean. Small lakes form and the river may flood over the countryside. The whole area is wet and muddy. A few trees, such as alder, grow here. Most of the land is covered by marshes and reeds.

At the mouth of the river, fresh water mixes with salt water. The wetlands around a river mouth also form marshy habitats. But as the river flows towards the ocean, the marshes become more salty.

Beneath the reeds, mud and peat slowly build up. This produces a rich soil for growing plants. In the past, most of the wetlands in Northern Europe were drained. They were used as farmland.

Among the Reedbeds

Ten animals that are out of place

1 Hippopotamus from Africa.

2 Sulfur-crested cockatoo from Australia.

3 Jacuna or lily trotter from North and South America.

4 Chameleon from forests in Madagascar.

5 Crab-eating macaque of Southeast Asia.

6 Florida panther from warm swampy areas in southern United States.

7 Shoe-billed stork from Africa.

8 Nile crocodile from North Africa.

9 Nile monitor is a large African lizard.

10 Ostrich from dry African grasslands.

Few areas of unspoiled marshland remain in Northern Europe. Many wetlands have been drained. Others are at risk. Many are now protected nature preserves. The mud and water help keep people and large predators from entering the marsh and harming the wildlife. The reed beds provide dense cover for animals to hide in.

Rare mammals like the European otter (A) and European mink (B) still survive in some marshes. They are both agile swimmers. The otter eats most things. It catches fish, crustaceans, and insects as well as birds, frogs, and baby rabbits. The European mink is very rare in some areas. It has been replaced by the American mink, which escaped from mink farms into the wild.

Coypu (C) are large ratlike rodents that first came from South America. They were raised on fur farms, but some escaped into the wild. They eat plant shoots. As they feed, their large teeth damage reed beds and riverbanks.

Wetlands are a special haven for waterbirds and waders. Mallards (D), moorhens (E), coots (F), and mute swans (G) live here. Gray herons (H) slowly wade in the water, looking for fish to catch. Marsh harriers (I) fly overhead in search of prey. In winter, the mudflats are home for migrating birds. Brent geese (J) spend the summer in the Arctic. They fly south to winter in the wetlands. Other birds just stop to rest on their migration flights north and south.

European wetlands

Europe's wetlands are at risk from farming, building, tourism, and watersports. Many, such as the Camargue in Southern France, are protected nature preserves. Others are not. Even the smallest patches of marsh need to be conserved for their natural wildlife. If wetlands continue to be drained and polluted, many of their plants and animals will die out.

Europe

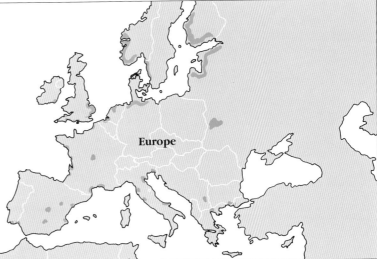

9

Tide Pools

Tide pools are puddles of water left on a rocky seashore when the tide goes out. Look closely at these two pictures of a tide pool on a North Atlantic beach. Can you spot the ten differences between them?

When the tide goes out on a rocky shore, water is trapped in pools. Some tide pools are tiny puddles, high up on the top of the rocks. Others, low on the shore, are huge, deep lagoons. Most are filled with many different seaweeds and animals. At low tide, animals left on the beach are in danger of drying out. In the tide pools, life continues as if the tide were in. A tide pool is a mini-view of life in shallow seas.

If you look into a tide pool, you will see many different animals. Anemones, chitons, mussels, and limpets cling to rocks. Periwinkles graze on the algae growing there.

Miniature Shallow Seas

Stinging tentacles circle the anemone's mouth. These stun their prey and then sweep it into the mouth. The limpet clings to the rocks very tightly. When a limpet moves, you can see a mark where it has been.

Hermit crabs and shore crabs hide in crevices or under ledges. The hermit crab is unusual. It does not have its own shell. Instead it lives in the cast-off shells of snails.

At the bottom of the pool, shrimp bury themselves in the sand. Tiny fish like the blenny hide beneath the rocks. Sometimes starfish like the brittlestar are stranded here, too.

Leaf worms and sea hares hide among the seaweed. The sea hare is a relative of a marine snail. It feeds on seaweed. It swims through the water using two flap-like "wings" at the side of its body. A sea cucumber lies on the bottom of the tide pool. A relative of the starfish, this strange animal spins long threads from its hind end. So its common name is the cotton spinner.

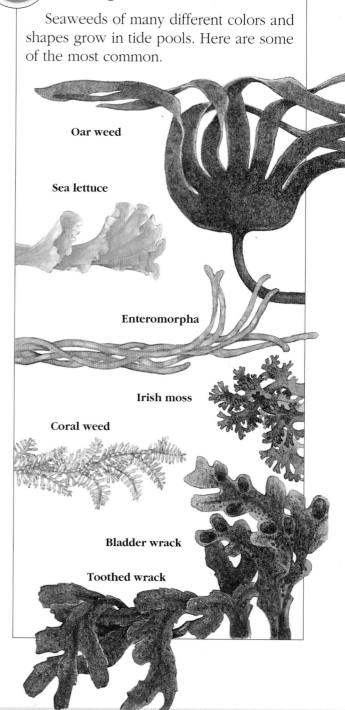

A garden of seaweeds

Seaweeds of many different colors and shapes grow in tide pools. Here are some of the most common.

Oar weed

Sea lettuce

Enteromorpha

Irish moss

Coral weed

Bladder wrack

Toothed wrack

The ten differences

1 A beadlet anemone's color has changed.

2 A shore crab's claw is open.

3 A common shrimp is now partly buried in the sand.

4 A limpet has moved. A groove in the rock, its resting place, is visible.

5 A gray chiton's shell now has only four plates.

6 There is another hermit crab in a periwinkle shell.

7 The blenny is hidden under a rock.

8 The sea cucumber has white threads coming from its hind end.

9 The sea hare's wings are a different shape.

10 The green leaf worm has moved from behind the seaweed.

Whose Baby?

Many planktonic animals in the ocean are the larvae, or young, of bottom-dwelling creatures. They are quite unlike their parents. Once they were thought to be totally different species. Look at the main picture of the plankton in the ocean. Can you match up each larva with its parent in the small pictures?

The animals that live in the plankton are often free-floating. Some can only make weak movements. Others can swim quite well. Many planktonic animals move up and down in the water with changes in daylight.

Some animals spend their whole lives in the plankton. Large numbers of free-swimming, shrimplike copepods live here. They are an important source of food for many fish.

Shallow coastal waters also contain the planktonic larvae of many animals. For example, barnacles, clams, crabs, starfish, sea snails, and some fish all have planktonic larvae.

In spring, millions of eggs are released into the ocean by many different sea creatures. These eggs are swept away on ocean currents. This happens in much the same way that some flower seeds are spread by the wind. The eggs hatch into larvae.

Planktonic copepods

Calanus is a free-swimming, shrimplike animal called a copepod. Their long, feathery antennae are very strong. They are used for swimming. Between the antennae is a single red eye. Although small, Calanus is an important sea creature because it is the main food of the herring.

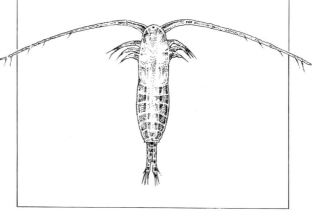

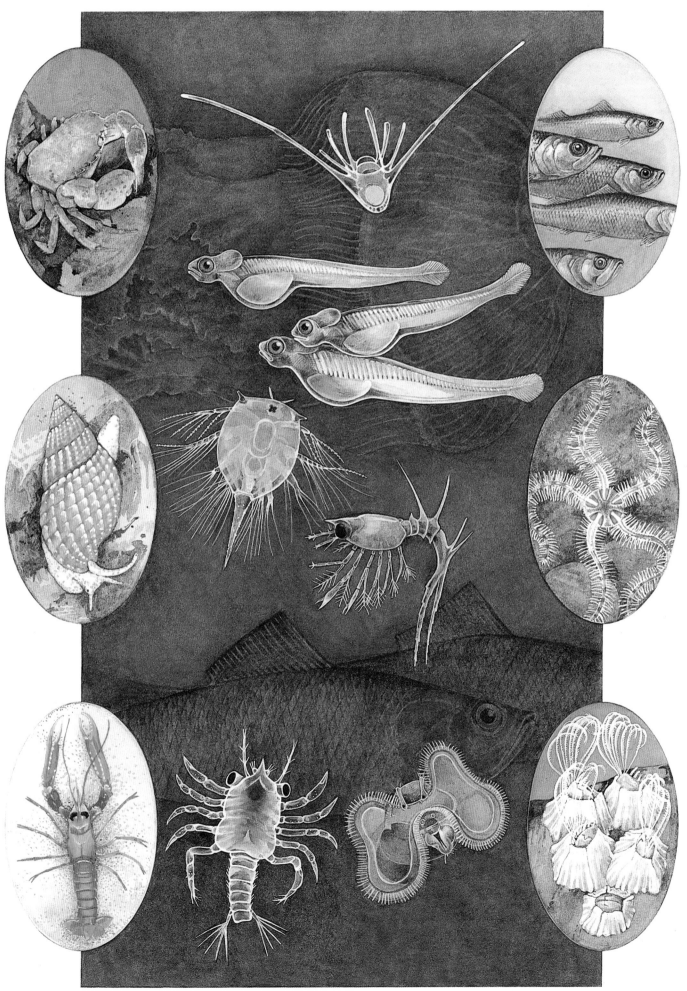

Floating Free

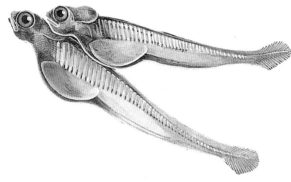

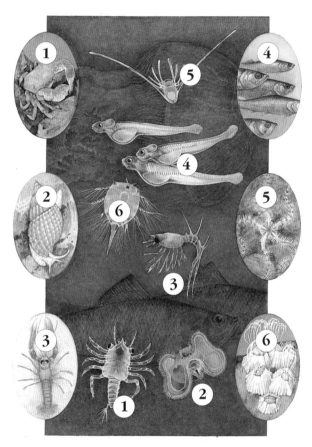

Match the parents and their larvae

1 Shore crab.
2 Dogwhelk.
3 Dublin Bay prawn (shrimp).
4 Herring.
5 Brittle star.
6 Acorn barnacle.

The newly hatched larvae are attracted to light. They move up to the ocean surface. They remain here for several weeks. Most of the larvae die before they become adults. Many are eaten by other animals.

Planktonic larvae have very light bodies to help them float. Many of them are see-through. Barnacle larvae swim using their long feathery arms. Crab and prawn larvae, such as the Dublin Bay prawn, have long spines that help them float. The delicate bodies of brittle star larvae have very long, stiff arms. The larvae of sea snails, such as the dogwhelk, do not have the heavy shells of their parents. Thin, fleshy wings spread out from their bodies. These are covered with tiny hairs called cilia.

Life cycle of a barnacle

Barnacles have two kinds of larvae. A barnacle's egg hatches into a floating planktonic larva. This first larva grows and develops into a second larva that can swim and crawl well. It swims down to the ocean floor to find the best place to settle as an adult. The larva becomes attached to a rock. Then it develops into an adult barnacle.

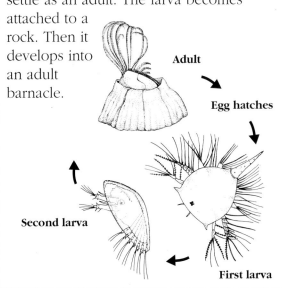

Adult

Egg hatches

Second larva

First larva

The cilia beat like rows of oars to move the larva along.

After many months of feeding and growing, the larvae reach the final stages of development. Many of them have changed shape. They now look more like the adults. The sea snails, such as the dogwhelk, have developed a shell and a foot.

At this stage, some of the larvae change their behavior. Larvae of animals that live on the ocean floor are attracted to the dark. They sink down to the bottom. Some, like prawns, crabs, and brittle stars, develop into free-moving adults. Others, like the acorn barnacle, will not move as adults. Their larvae now enter a swimming and seeking stage. They search for the perfect place to spend their life as adults. This search is very important for animals that will not move again.

Adult barnacles spend their lives stuck to a rock. Once the larva settles, it cannot move. So it must choose the best place to survive. Adult barnacles help the larva by releasing a chemical into the water. This attracts the young to settle near the adults.

Many fish larvae also live in the plankton. Herring eggs are laid in a mass of jelly attached to stones or seaweed. They hatch after about ten days. The young fish float up to the plankton. They cannot swim and have a large egg sac as a store of food. Herring larvae eat smaller planktonic animals. They slowly grow into the adult fish. Adult herrings prey on larger planktonic animals such as copepods. In turn, herring are food for larger fish, whales, birds, and people.

Glossary

Aerial root A special root produced by some trees that live in water. These roots help the plant to take in oxygen from the air.

Alga (plural **algae**) A group of plantlike living things. Many algae live in salt and fresh water.

Burrow A tunnel that many kinds of animals dig in the ground. Some animals live in their burrows. Others just use them to find food, sleep in, or as a nest for their young.

Camouflage The trait of blending in with the background.

Colony (plural **colonies**) A group of living things of the same kind that live together.

Detritus The remains of rotting animals and plants. It provides food for many living things.

Estuary The broad mouth of a river where the fresh water mixes with salt water.

Gonads The parts of an animal's body that make the male or female sex cells.

Habitat The place in which an animal or plant lives. Habitats include deserts, rain forests, grassland, mountains, and seashores. Each type of animal or plant is best suited to one or a few habitats.

Larva (plural **larvae**) The young of certain animals, such as frogs, crustaceans, some insects, and some fish. A larva hatches from the egg and often looks quite different from its parents.

Nymph The young form of some types of insects, such as dragonflies and grasshoppers.

Plankton Microscopic living things that float near the surface of the ocean and freshwater lakes.

Polyp A hollow, cup-shaped animal with a ring of tentacles around its mouth.

Predator An animal that kills and eats other animals.

Prey An animal that is killed and eaten by another animal.

Sonar The way an animal finds its way by using sound waves. Many animals, such as whales, make high-pitched noises. These bounce back off objects in their path. These sounds are also used to communicate with other animals.

Species A group of animals or plants that all look similar. They can mate with each other to produce young.

Stilt root A special type of root produced by some plants. The roots help to support the main stem or trunk.

Territory (plural **territories**) An area of land or water in which an animal, or group of animals, lives.

Index

A Templar Book

Devised and produced by The Templar Company plc
Pippbrook Mill, London Road, Dorking, Surrey RH4 1JE, Great Britain
© Copyright 1996 by The Templar Company plc